PRAISE for *eat the glitter*

Kat Dixon is the opposite of bor
glitter is poetry as conceptual ar
language with wit and intelligen
loved it.
— Clare Pollard

GW00776309

Kat Dixon's attention to the world is deep, sharp and unafraid.
What's seen is vivid, what's said is exact, and the mad masks make
perfect sense. The slashes and gaps do fine work too, punctuating
time with gasps and glances, as the wounded heart and soul face
down the nonsense of the life we have now. A superb debut from a
richly gifted witness.
— Glyn Maxwell

Kat Dixon's poems are about the stuff of modern life – relationships,
sex, technology, advertising. They are resolutely urban, set in clubs,
barbershops, galleries – places of congregation and complication.
They are found, redacted, torn up and reconstructed. She evokes
the spirit of Yoko Ono, imploring us to make our own art from
our unreal post-Covid times. Dixon's is a wholly original and
compelling voice, and *eat the glitter* is the kind of debut that makes
you sit up and take notice.
— Tamar Yoseloff

eat the glitter is a smart and stylish pamphlet that, appropriately
enough, sparkles with wit and formal inventiveness. But Kat
Dixon isn't just concerned with linguistic flourishes and striking
images, beneath this razzle-dazzle surface, there is an invigorating
emotional frankness to these poems, particularly the ones that
explore the body and desire.

Dixon isn't scared of holding back, even when it comes to
exposing her own vulnerabilities. And it is this glorious mix, the
bold, the beautiful and the dangerously exposed, that makes *eat the
glitter* such a rich poetry treat.
— Emma Simon

eat the glitter

Kat Dixon (she/her) is a queer writer living in London. Her poetry has appeared in *The Rialto, Butcher's Dog, Queerlings, Mslexia, fourteenpoems, ReCreation Anthology, Spectrum Anthology,* and various publications. Her work has been shortlisted and commended for various prizes, including the Café Writers Prize, Ver Prize, Rialto Pamphlet Prize, and Mslexia single poem prize. She has an MA in Writing Poetry with Newcastle University and The Poetry School.

ISBN: 978-1-916938-23-6

Cover designed by Aaron Kent

Edited and Typeset by Aaron Kent

Broken Sleep Books Ltd
PO BOX 102
Llandysul
SA44 9BG

CONTENTS

DRIPS IN A BUCKET   9

DEAR ARTS COUNCIL   10

OPEN TABS ON A LAPTOP, 2.38AM   11

THIS LETTER CONSTITUTES A FORMAL RELATIONSHIP   12

PSYCHOTHERAPY FOR BEGINNERS   14

IDRIS   15

PRO / CON   16

KIND TO HANDS KILLS 99.9% OF BACTERIA   18

EXPLORE OUR COLLAGEN BONE BROTH   19

I DON'T LEAK I FLOOD   20

FUCK / PERFUME ADS   21

LESSONS IN FLAGELLATION   22

AS IN   24

NORWAY   25

(POLY)GRAMMATICAL GYMNASTICS   26

FUCK / WHITE PRIVILEGE   27

A WHITE BRANCH EXPLOSION   28

SKIN AS PROTECTIVE LAYER   30

CONFERENCE ROOM B FOR A LITANY OF HUMAN FAILURES   31

THE FRAME IS OFFENSIVELY ORNATE AND THERE'S NOWHERE TO
CRY IN THE TATE   32

INSTRUCTIONS   34

ACKNOWLEDGEMENTS   37

eat the glitter

Kat Dixon

Broken Sleep Books

DRIPS IN A BUCKET

we're in a beer garden on Blackhorse Road / with these massive glasses / gin glasses / and you're talking about gay icons and Jacqueline Wilson and how Ellie from those Girls in Love books was definitely gay / and I say / what / how was she / and you point out the bit when she sleeps next to her best friend / smells her hair / talking about the curve of her best friend's spine / and I'm a bit drunk / squiffy my Mum would call it / and I say / yeah / but I felt that way / about some of my friends / thinking about Celeste / her strawberry blonde hair / down her back / soft skin / round the base of her breasts / when we got changed for P.E. / her white legs / when we got changed to go out / playing rounds of pool in the cine-complex / chasing boys / we kissed once / scent of damp grass and wet trainers / in a tent on a school trip / boys watching / all eyes on us / heat of fascination / and I didn't want the kiss to stop / the ice in your gin glass is melting / you've taken your sunglasses off / you're watching me / sucking on your lime / the traffic nearby feels suddenly close and far away / and I say / I can't believe Ellie was gay / poor Ellie / not knowing all this time

Dear Arts Council / I've been thinking
about potentially starting some work
can you help? / I'd like to buy a fine bag
of mescaline / a finger's lick of DMT
the outputs / might possibly be
a life-sized replica of Pinochet
a sculpture made of dinosaur bones
or a book / do you have a Navel Gazing Fund?
I'd like to get weird / look deep into my tissues
pour my eyeballs / into a bowl of chef's knives
what eligibility criteria applies? I need that
six-month break / from paying rent
for Twitter / to burn down
there is genius / pooling in my elbows
my opus / just out of reach
if only I could sit still / for more than half an hour
do you think Kant wanked / this much?
be a love / stuff some cash in an envelope
whack on a stamp / I swear / I'll spend it good

OPEN TABS ON A LAPTOP, 2.38AM

Can insomnia kill you? | Therapy.org
How to fall asleep in 10, 20 or 60 seconds | healthline.com
Rachel (@racheyface) | Instagram.com

How much should millennials have saved by age 30? | Forbes.com
When is a Headache a Sign of a Brain Tumor? | blog.dana-farber.com
Rachel Stone | Facebook.com

Rachel Stone | LinkedIn.com
Rachel Stone (@rachinyourface) | Tiktok.com
Rachel Stone | @therachplace | Pinterest.com

How to get over an ex: 10+ ways to get your life back on track | eharmony.com
What to do if you accidentally like someone's pic | joeblog.co.uk
Online dating advice: 11 ways to win at Tinder | metro.co.uk

How to mine Bitcoin: Everything you need to know | cointelegraph.com
What is the "Free Britney" movement? | harpersbazaar.com
7 Small ways to improve your relationship with your Mom | mindbodygreen.com

Rachel (@rachplaceforever) | Twitter.com
Can insomnia kill you? | Therapy.org
Tall quiet blondes | YouPorn.com

THIS LETTER CONSTITUTES A FORMAL RELATIONSHIP

1.1.   We are delighted to enter into the relationship. This letter constitutes a formal agreement, binding from from ███████, the Parties' first date.

1.2.   All publicity, including social media, must be jointly agreed by both Parties in line with co-branding principles.

    1.2.1.   No reckless tweets.

    1.2.2.   Unflattering photographs are banned.

1.3.   Both Parties retain the right to rifle through pockets.

1.4.   All data shared between Parties must be kept confidential in accordance with the Data Protection Act 2018.

    1.4.1.   Items include but not limited to:

        1.4.1.1.   reciprocal pet names;

        1.4.1.2.   the chocolate gateau recipe;

        1.4.1.3.   the tenderness of seeing each other in grief.

    '

1.5.   Both Parties retain the right to a cheeky snog, should a high school crush, Malibu cocktails or ████ appear from nowhere.

1.6.   The Relationship should not be copied or imitated in future relationships without prior written consent.

    1.6.1.   Current items subject to Intellectual Property conditions include:

        1.6.1.1.   listening while not listening;

        1.6.1.2.   discreetly disposing of ugly clothing;

        1.6.1.3.   the towel dance that always made them laugh;

1.6.1.4.   and ████████████.

1.7.   Both Parties enjoy parties. Each Party may
       attend a party without the other Party should the
       aforementioned Party be moody, badly dressed or hate
       their friends.

1.8.   All ████ must be ████ without any further ████ due to
       aforementioned ██████████████████████████
       █████████████████████

1.9.   Both Parties retain the right to check their dating Apps.
       Just in case.

PSYCHOTHERAPY FOR BEGINNERS

for three years, I met with a man in a small, carpeted room
& gently, I learned how to live with myself

some textbooks call it integration. other words:
attachment, kindness, love

a breakthrough moment; session 72, I accused
the black & white geometric rug of giving me a headache

next week the rug had been folded & tucked to one side
we kept the window slightly ajar, in case one of us needed to jump

I calculated on my phone how much I'd spent
the phone landed with a thunk, but didn't break

real relationships can sustain fracture & repair
the lamp in the corner was beige

how many people in your life are paid to move a rug?
how many people move a rug out of love?

a mature perspective sees multiple sides.
truisms are true & truly out of reach until we reach them

I mourn the minutes. sometimes a rug is love
sometimes a rug is just a rug

IDRIS

every time I walk in / that slow acceptance / same row of leather chairs / pots of combs / hey man / hey / how's it been / slotting straight back in / low rumble of flat chat / shared ease / swipe a eucalyptus flannel from the steamer / hold the corners / swing in tight spirals / tight nods / something about witness / we speak into mirrors / eyes lock / fingertip smiles / tino is playing disco on the stereo again / and every now and then / kane does a little dance / grab a corona straight out the fridge / strategic swigs / bottles slick / cylinders of wax / smells like a fresh hand slap / click the headrest / swivel me round / lean me back into the most intimate / my head in your hands / water nestling scalp / brief / safety / surrender / over in a flash slap of flesh / razorslick / here's the back / mirror to mirror / and I'm laughing at matt's dad jokes / rows of plants / lines of scissors / shavers / towels / half-drunk can of coke / and at the desk / my hand passes over witchcraft contactless / fist bump / fist bump / see you next time yeah / and my smile / follows me out into the street

PRO / CON

PRO	CON
agonisingly good-looking	talks when I'm talking
great in bed	velcro wallet
listens and remembers things I've said	believes in free market economics
quick wit	always late
reliably high quality coke	cuts his toenails in the bedroom
introduced me to salmon skin sushi	can't stand that I earn more than he does
free gig tickets	considers feminism solved

16

rubs my hands when it's cold

says *your pussy is beautiful*

asks my opinion on existential questions

makes me laugh through my nose

calls me his *favourite*

adores me

said he could really fall in love with me

thinks my vulva is a Gameboy

skilled in lies of omission

spilled beer on my baby blue sweater

broke my grandmother's mug

calls me his *favourite*

hit me

didn't

KIND TO HANDS KILLS 99.9% OF BACTERIA

WARNING: Highly flammable. Direct contact may cause irritation. Long stretches without human interaction can lead to low mood, hermit behaviours, a desperate need for touch. If contact occurs rinse immediately with therapy.

Keep container tightly closed. Do not allow emotions to flow in or out. Keep out of reach of children.

INGREDIENTS: Alcohol, Aqua, Glycerin, C-10-30, Confusion, Alkyl Acrylate Crosspolymer, Proponal, Leaf Extract, Yearning.

Kind to Hands takes no legal responsibility for ingested product, inflammation or compulsive weeping.

If swallowed, seek medical advice. Keep your fears to yourself.

EXPLORE OUR COLLAGEN BONE BROTH

I'm inviting you to source breath
Tell me your passwords
Pass me your tell words
Eat beautiful for £4.29

I'm telling you to dream fresh
Organic smoothie matters
Kiwi skins and broken flesh
Ask us about our eggs

I'm filtering your small fears
Plant-based oxytocin, right here
We will keep you safe
Walk don't run this way

I'm helping you to want well
Clear your exit, carb less
Assemble your points
Discover authentic keto breath

I DON'T LEAK I FLOOD

Yesterday, on a date, I tore off my face.
There are many ways, wet slap of blood on thrusted cunt,
to make arterial splatter. White sheets are clichéd,

but there I was, standing in his miniature bathroom,
foaming up hand soap, scrubbing his sheets, face dripping. Blood
forms a brown cloud-edge, the beginning of a stain. I'd wrecked

my face, tore strips of nose, shredded cheeks, splayed chunks
of breast and pubic hair across his half-sized bed. I hate it when
people don't hang up their towels, that musty stench.

Then, of course, I was worried about his sheets. Congealed
vulva lips and all the multitudinous ways that a liquid leak
is not okay. Fortunately, I am a well-trained woman.

When rage boils and my body explodes, shrieks of shredded skin
under a fingernail's dark trail, I know all about cold water
and the properties of soap. I have scrubbed my face

from many duvet sets, rinsed out bio-matter shards of shame,
cleaned myself from the splattered blast zone.
And here is his sheet, ready for the next. White again.

FUCK / *PERFUME ADS*

After Inua Ellams

she wakes in a wide-angle bed / white sheets / sequinned dress
/ jump cut / her ass bent over a dual-tone motorbike / engine
growls / pan past the Louvre / she turns / orders coffee in French
/ sips / smashes the white espresso cup / lip juts / jump cut /
she's riding a horse / night lit / the horse orders coffee in French
/ phosphorescence glitters on the beach / sand flies under hooves
/ mane flying / hair flying / she leans back on the bed / she's got
a galaxy in her cunt / sheer curtains flail / the knight in chain mail
runs through a forest glade / wet leaves / soft fade / a tree lifts its
branch / spanks her ass / zoom high through the stars / pass the
motorbike / on fire / the knight runs by / on fire / the black in her
eyes becomes a pool of night sky / hold it / scan the tracker back /
rewatch / how can I want / this scene / how can I both laugh and
want / why do I want / to ride that motorbike / look back over her
bare shoulder / eyes to mine / look back over her bare shoulder /
again / again

LESSONS IN FLAGELLATION

(1)

An ingrown hair is one that has grown back into its follicle. An ingrown hair is one that is returning to the body.

I've heard women say there are few things more satisfying than removing an ingrown hair. Lift the error, flick it out. One woman I know spent hundreds of pounds on laser surgery to have hair on and around her vulva permanently removed.

If a standard wax costs twenty-five quid (once every three to four weeks), a woman who waxes spends approximately ten thousand pounds on waxes in her lifetime. That's a third of the fees of an MBA at a decent London business school.

There are several favoured positions for getting your anus waxed. (1) The lotus (2) holding your feet above your head (3) face down, pulling your bum cheeks apart.

(2)

The hip has a good line of darkness around it. A stabilising object during sex. A signifier that you've space to store a foetus.

(3)

Porn has become democratised. No more Victorian etchings or peeking over Picasso's balcony. Want to get off? youporn.com, instantly. Anywhere with a satellite link.

If porn equates to 30% of server storage across global internet usage, and the average server uses 1200 kilowatts per hour, porn use accounts for approximately 0.7% of global energy consumption.

This celebration of democratic access falters in the face of (1) fourteen year olds getting paid $8 per photo on OnlyFans, (2) the loneliness of camgirls, (3) pre-teens presenting at UK GP surgeries with anal fissures.

(4)

I'm told I have a 'porn-sized' arse. Like most women, I occasionally wish bits of myself into non-existence.

Over gins, a friend tells me she'd rather sweat through a light grey shirt than show her bare arms in public.

AS IN

After Sakinah Hofler

more calls to helplines, as in two months after celebrating his
twenty-first birthday, as in

massively struggled, as in I just wish he'd have held on, as in

access to support services, both online and in person, as in these
situations, lots of gay people, families who don't accept them, as in

44% increase in calls to helplines, we loved and supported him,
as in coroner not required to log data on sexual orientation or
gender identity, as in

11,000 people have accessed suicide prevention, he had so much
ahead of him, as in government officials, as in

we are absolutely committed to supporting everyone's mental
health, especially during this unprecedented period, as in

not counting means the struggle will continue for others, as in

we loved and supported him, I just wish he'd held on

NORWAY

you're on a boat with a woman you're supposed to love   trees
grow out of the mountain   waterfalls are high huge strong   the
boat draws close so that you   the woman you're supposed to love
the strangers you are sharing this experience with   can reach out
fill a glass of water   you take photos   you reach over the side
fill a glass of water   out here it's impossible to ignore   flecks of
water on the camera lens   you drink the water   exclaim how
fresh it tastes   you've never tasted water so fresh   her body is
facing towards the mountains   her body is facing away from you
the water is really very fresh   Debbie from Canada says she won't
be able to drink the water back home   now she's tasted this   the
glasses aren't glasses   they are made from single use plastic   for
all the people who did this before   for all the people who will do
this after you   a man gets the zip caught on his mac   his wife
helps him   she is a barrister from Maine   when is your lover not
your lover   the engines are loud against the mountains   if the
mountains could shake they would shake

(POLY)GRAMMATICAL GYMNASTICS

you is a useful term because it is singular and plural
they is a useful term because it is singular and plural

> for the sake of two teas and a coffee on Sunday morning
> for the sake of three croissants and happier than I'd felt in years

say *you* in Russian / say *they* in Croatian / say *us* and say
almost nothing, an almost unnoticeable something

> for the sake of a sentence, for the end-of-meeting chat
> for the sake of clients, for the sake of simplicity

girlfriend was easier at work (also true / also not true)
deeply closeted but slightly closer to saying something

> for the sake of not drawing a triangle and a T shape on a napkin
> and getting into the history of multiplicity

couldn't say *they* with *you* (felt like stealing) quietly tucked away
presenting differently everywhere we went

> *it's a bit like coming out as gay ten years ago, isn't it*
> *maybe it'll be more normal in future*

perhaps all my love letters to you are inherently confused
inherently a *you* that is not accommodated by our language

> for the sake of being, for the sake of not having to explain
> some days it's just harder to take up space

FUCK / *WHITE PRIVILEGE*

After Inua Ellams

last night you asked me / where my skin is from / and I didn't have an answer to hand / this question spans / a few centuries / next week a man will stare at us in a café / and I will be surprised / be embarrassed by my surprise / here in this space / with a duvet and yesterday's coffee / and the sweet smell of rubbed bodies / I don't have my antennae switched on / but you do / always / this is the price it would seem / that I get to relax / the facts are not important until they are / I got the country wrong / where you're from / and again it seems this is one of those things / I've borrowed / my ignorance spread on morning toast / poured into potholes / who knew going for a walk was a white girl thing / let me breathe into this discomfort / please / tell me what you need / wait no / I was trying to unpick / and this is where I should be / standing on the corner of your street / knowing every mangled bush / bicycle frame / car wash sign / and not know anything / not knowing a fucking thing / I promise / this is where I will be

A WHITE BRANCH EXPLOSION

we drank what we could find / slices of lime and unanswerable questions
like how many would die and how long would this last

streets held themselves empty / pub windows boarded up
I considered what it meant to breathe / I considered small amounts of drugs

I considered / blossom

to make cardamom buns the proper way you have to break cardamom pods with a knife
we'd been inside & we understood inside but we understood nothing

adequacy took on a new meaning / the buns took four hours to prove
living felt untested but deeply familiar / people walked their dogs slowly at night

cinnamon tastes bitter straight from the spoon / other people's problems were both upsetting and far away

my flatmate threw away the leftover buns / in the darker moments / I hated her for it

I feared we were losing something fundamental / I feared something had gone beyond none of it was real / and we would never get back what we lost

dabbing MDMA on a Sunday is something like a bad patch
cinnamon blended with flour / tastes like dry wood / varnish rubbed clean

I found / I could only write about it in past tense
blossom collected on pavements / blossom collected on trees

wherever we looked / eyes sparkling wide / blossom

SKIN AS PROTECTIVE LAYER

things I let out: sweat, carbon dioxide, pus, discharge, platelets
(see how close platelets are to planets?) tears, froth, laughter, drool

things I let in: semen, dihydrogen monoxide, gin, tiny pork
dumplings, oxygen, unnecessary fears, blood (have you ever
licked someone's menses in a shower cubicle? the way brown
blood falls apart under the water's flow?), cactus spines, bacteria,
cat hair, dirt

things I let out: distrust, confusion, sneezes, impatience, the
animal sense of being ejected from the pack, farts, coughs, the
occasional mucus spatter

things I let in: other people's emotions, panic, that advert on the
tube that always makes me yawn (are you tired of being tired?)
secretions of love, strap-ons, unhappy marriages, flies (I pulled
a spider off my face once in my sleep, it crunched under my
fingertips), plant leaves, scud, flickers of tension between my
parents, seawater, grit, giggling, soap

CONFERENCE ROOM B FOR A LITANY OF HUMAN FAILURES

A woman holds out sunflower seeds and wishes
the man standing in front of her would die.

When my hands hurt, I plunge them into plastic bowls
of ice water and watch them turn white. Joints shriek.

Rolling a cigarette has degrees of success. A common
failure is letting the filter get wet with your spit.

The power of a right hook comes from your hips
not your fists. Imagine it's his head. Imagine it's his head.

Child abuse is most prevalent amongst families who struggle
for money. Neglect can be not feeding a child, not giving a child a hug.

The difference between gaming and gambling is most apparent
in legal & regulatory frameworks. To a 14-year-old, it feels the same.

I had too many meetings this week about the world being shit.
An excess of reality kills hope.

A woman with sunflower seeds can be a solider. A woman
with sunflowers seeds can be a handful of hope

THE FRAME IS OFFENSIVELY ORNATE AND THERE'S NOWHERE TO CRY IN THE TATE

She's hugging a man with a hole for a face
Many times, lately, it seems like mustard yellow horizons
are getting closer

Behind her, there's a building that was once a fortress
A building that once felt safe, and a seagull
making shadows by the cliffs

What's important is the man with the hole for a face
has a quill on his shoulder, which is symbolic
A quill is always symbolic

Her face is in the crook of his neck
because it feels like safety, because it is safety
or as close as we ever get

A shaft of light brings my eyes to her backside
which makes me think she was painted
by a man

I am resisting talking about it
but I still am, like a burn on a map, or a magnet in a bowl of blades
or a rape

The man with a hole in his face has a hole above his crotch too
through which I can see the beginnings of a
mustard yellow horizon

Is it me? Is it her? Were we supposed to check that he was whole?

A crook of a neck is as close as we ever get

The seagull calls

INSTRUCTIONS

After Yoko Ono

Cough into your elbow crease.
Watch it fill with glitter.
Eat the glitter.

Ask strangers if they understand their mask.
Slice open a lemon & sniff hard.
Hug yourself.

Queue gently.
Rub alcohol gel into your vulva.
Piss in parks.

Lick alcohol gel off your hands.
Vomit in sixty second intervals.
Tell no one.

Hold your face mask in your left hand.
Use it to strain peas.
Make soup.

Twang the elastic of your face mask with your ear.
Listen to weeks slip by.
Eat rain.

Rub alcohol gel into your thighs.
Eat swordfish on the sly.
Clap.

Try not to drink your hand gel like a vodka shot.

Try not to brush anyone's skin.

Try not to want.

ACKNOWLEDGEMENTS

Thanks are due to the editors of the following magazines and publications in which some of these poems first appeared: *fourteen poems, Queerlings, New Boots and Pantisocracies, Ink Sweat & Tears, Mslexia*, and *Re:Creation Anthology*.

'The frame is offensively ornate and there's nowhere to cry in the Tate' was highly commended in the Ver Poets Open Competition 2022. 'Instructions' was a finalist in the Mslexia 2020 Poetry Competition.

I want to thank Newcastle University and The Poetry School for awarding me a scholarship for the MA Writing Poetry programme – this gifted me a massive leap forward. Thanks to all the staff and teachers at The Poetry School, especially Andy Parkes, for making brilliant poetry classes accessible. You've helped me learn so much.

Special thanks go to Tamar Yoseloff and Glyn Maxwell, for their unwavering belief, support and insightful teaching. You've both been incredible.

Thank you Nathan Evans and Justin David – you both came to my first poetry reading and, years later, you gave me my first big performance on stage. Thank you.

Thank you to my poetry communities, for the laughter, the critique and the support. Special thanks to the MA class of 2021 (and the years above and below) for sharing the journey and having such a blast together along the way.

Thank you to those who read early versions of these poems, especially Emma Simon, Vanessa Lampert, Anne Symons and Sara Levy. Special thanks to Vanessa for generously offering to proof read.

Thank you to every writer I have shared moments with at Gladstone's Library, and the staff that run the retreat house. This pamphlet would not exist without that special space.

Thank you to my publisher, Aaron, for such an enjoyable process.

To Katie, Jeremy, Ben, Ana, Eleanor and Ugo, who show up, send exclamation marks and continue to cheer me on.

Finally, and most importantly, thank you to my Mum and Dad, who've unendingly supported my writing. You whoop down the phone every time I get something published and you beam in the crowd at my readings. Your support is very special. Thank you.

LAY OUT YOUR UNREST

Milton Keynes UK
Ingram Content Group UK Ltd.
UKHW012253150624
444183UK00001B/5

9 781916 938236